Six Socks for Six Feet

Written by Samantha Montgomerie

Illustrated by Sakshi Mangal

Collins

Buzz is a hip hop bee.

He needs his fox socks. Fox socks rock!

Buzz sighs.

His room is a mess of socks!

Six sheep socks zoom into the box.

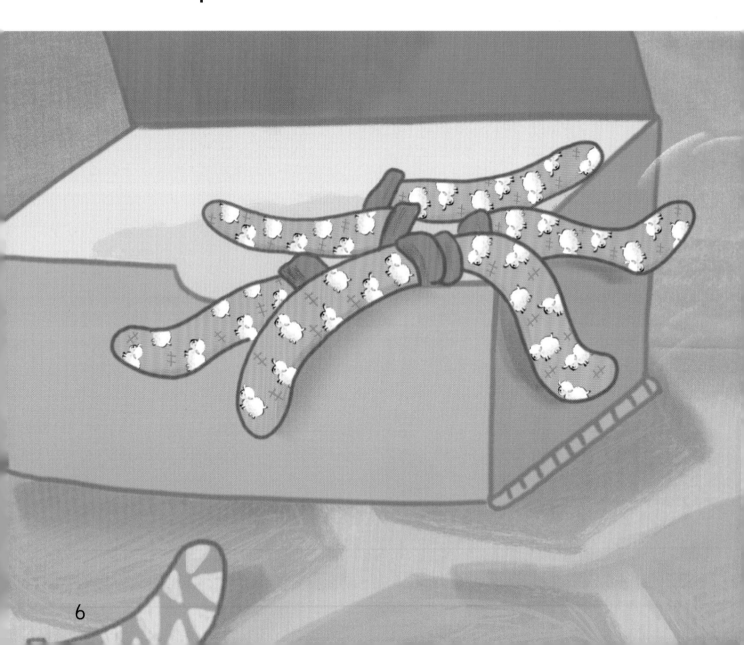

Six goat socks go in too.

In go shark socks, cow socks ...

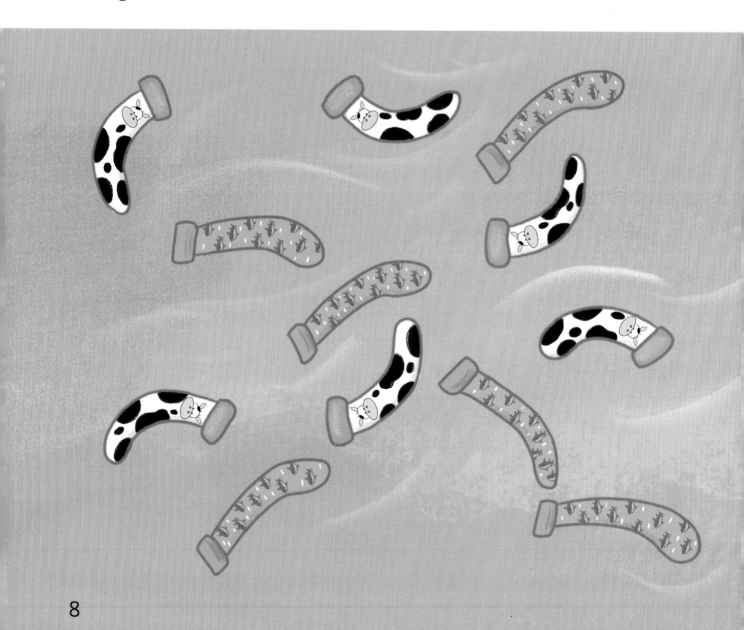

rabbit socks and popcorn socks.

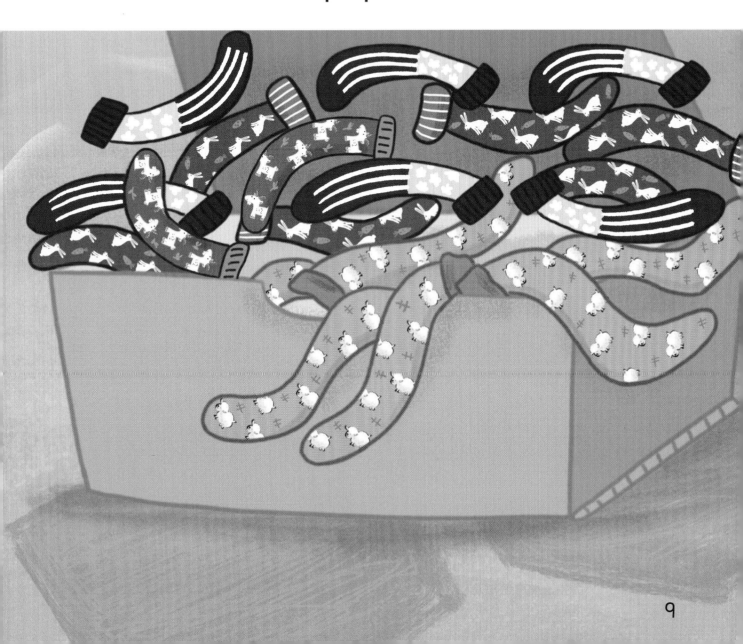

Buzz sees a pair hidden under the bed.

Buzz joins the hip hop bees.

He kicks his feet in his fox socks.

Six socks for Buzz

🐾 Review: After reading 🐾

Use your assessment from hearing the children read to choose any GPCs, words or tricky words that need additional practice.

Read 1: Decoding

- On pages 2 and 3, ask: Why do the fox socks **rock**? (e.g. *because they're colourful; because they're perfect for a pop star*). Talk about other meanings of "rock". Prompt with phrases such as: a rock star; a mountain rock; rock a baby.
- Focus on the grapheme "oo". On pages 5, 6 and 7, ask the children to point to an "oo" and sound out the word. (*room, zoom, too*)
- On page 11, point to **look**. Ask: Does this have the same /oo/ sound or is it different? (*it's a short /**oo**/, not a long /oo/*) Encourage the children to sound it out and compare it with the long /oo/ sound.
- Model reading page 10 slowly and fluently. Challenge the children to read it too. Say: Can you blend in your head when you read these words?

Read 2: Prosody

- Challenge the children to read pages 4 and 5 like a storyteller.
- On page 4, discuss how Buzz feels and why he sighs. Challenge the children to read the page in a sad tone, like a sigh.
- On page 5, ask: What feeling should we show when we read this? Prompt by pointing to the exclamation mark and saying that this page is explaining a big problem. Encourage the children to read the page dramatically.

Read 3: Comprehension

- Ask the children which of Buzz's socks they liked best. Ask: If you could have any design on a pair of socks, what would you choose?
- Focus on the character of Buzz. Say: What do you know about him? Prompt with questions such as: Is he tidy? How do you know? What kind of music does he like?
- Encourage the children to retell the story using the pictures on pages 14 and 15 as prompts. Ask: What has Buzz lost? (*his fox socks*) What sort of socks has he got? (e.g. *goat, shark, cow*) What is under the bed? (*the fox socks*) What happens in the end? (e.g. *he dances with his fox socks on*)